Behold Your King

31 Reflections on the Gospel of Matthew

By Catherine Warwick

Edited by Julie McKiddie

FOREWORD

I am very pleased to introduce the author of this devotional book to you. My Mom, Catherine Warwick, taught Bible Study Fellowship in Wilmington, North Carolina for 15 years. She would say that it was one of the highlights of her life.

Mom loved God's Word, and she loved researching and learning. Because of those passions, she was an excellent teacher whose goal was to excite others to study and search God's Word also.

My daughter, Julie McKiddie, has that same love and passion for God's Word and teaching. She has spent many hours poring over Mom's lectures from the book of Matthew. She has compiled segments of those teachings into a devotional book meant to inspire you with a fresh vision of Jesus Christ as King of Kings and Lord of Lords.

The hope and desire of the authors is to pass along a legacy of love for our Lord Jesus and His Word. Please read the passages in Matthew and the devotion that corresponds to each Scripture. Allow God's Spirit to teach you. Open your heart to know and love your King, Jesus.

- Carol Stertzer

PREFACE

Many women attend church or a weekday Bible study, but sadly not many of those gatherings are actually centered around God's Word. As a result, there are self-proclaimed Christian women who do not really understand who Jesus is or what it means to be a part of his Kingdom. This devotional presents Christ-centered teaching from the book of Matthew - infusing fresh vision of who Christ is and propelling us to bow our knees to his good and righteous rule in our lives.

Submission to any authority is a point of tension and even confusion for many. We tend to think democracy and shared authority are much preferable. But as we study this Gospel, you will come to see that submitting to Jesus, the King of all Kings, is the only way to truly live. Jesus does not beat around the bush when he describes the challenges that face his followers, but he is also clear about the reward.

Many of us have a misconstrued idea of what kind of a King God is. We see him as distant, foreboding, or exacting – like the unapproachable King in his far off castle. We think that if he did want anything to do with us, it certainly wouldn't be something we would want him to do. We need a better understanding of God's true nature. We need to know our King. So, we will focus on Jesus in Matthew's Gospel to learn from the only One who knows perfectly what our Heavenly Father is like. Jesus proclaimed, "Whoever has seen me has seen the Father" (John 14:9). Matthew wrote that we might believe that Jesus is the promised Messiah of the Old Testament and therefore obey him as King. Our study is not so much for information, but transformation. To know him better is to love him more and desire to be more like him, which we are told is the will of the Father for us. Let us invite him to take a close look at us and obediently cooperate with him as he changes us from the inside out.

These daily devotions are meant to be read after reading the Scripture listed for each day. Please take time to read the passage first so that you have in mind the full context of what Jesus said or did. Then, the devotional will take you deeper into that text, helping you understand it and apply it to your life.

The author of these devotions is my grandmother. She went to be with Jesus in April 2013 after many years of following him. She loved God's Word, and she loved to share it with others. One of her great joys was being a teaching leader for Bible Study Fellowship in Wilmington, North Carolina. These devotions are compiled from her teaching manuscripts for BSF. It was an immense privilege and a pleasure to be taught by her again as I edited this book, and I commend it to you. I pray that the Holy Spirit will capture your heart as you read and give you a renewed vision of our King and what it means to advance His Kingdom by the power of His Spirit.

Day 1 – Trusting God's Plan A
Matthew 1:18-25

This wasn't part of his plan. In fact, it seemed quite the opposite. We can imagine how Joseph's heart must have broken when he learned of Mary's pregnancy. Yet, he was sympathetic toward her, and his actions showed how much he loved her. He loved her with a love that went beyond the letter of the law, which pronounced stoning for this offense. Not wanting to shame her publicly or bring about her death, he decided to divorce her in secret. Then, the Lord appeared and redirected him.

We are often confused by events in our lives. Because our vision is limited, we might fail to see Divine movement. God's ways are too vast and wonderful for our understanding.

In this instance, God sent an angel to help Joseph understand his ways, and the angel said, "Do not fear." This is perhaps one of the most tender commands that the Lord gives in Scripture. Is he speaking that word to you today? *Do not be afraid. I know what you see. Let me help you by giving you my perspective.* In Isaiah 55:8-9, he tells his people, "For my thoughts are not your thoughts, neither are your ways my ways, declares the Lord. For as the heavens are higher than the earth, so are my ways higher than your ways and my thoughts than your thoughts."

The angel told Joseph that Mary had not been unfaithful. The child was of the Holy Spirit, not of another man. What a revelation for Joseph! We can only imagine what he felt. Amazement. Relief. Gratitude. He could take his beloved Mary as his wife, and he would also be given the care of God's own Son.

In light of what Joseph was told, and because he knew God's Word, he believed. "When Joseph woke from sleep, he did as the angel of the Lord commanded him: he took his wife, but knew her not until she had given birth to a son. And he called his name Jesus" (Matthew 1:24-25). Immediate and complete obedience.

Are you willing to obey right away, even if you don't have all the facts? In instances where others may not understand and may ridicule you? Is God asking you to do something that defies human reason or threatens your well-laid plans?

Mary and Joseph knew God and had faith in His Word. They were sensitive and heard when he spoke to them. They were willing to be obedient – immediately and without full disclosure.

This is a beautiful example for you and me. When we take steps of faith in obedience to God's Word, we may not always know what will happen, but we have the promise that Jesus is Emmanuel – God with us, no matter what.

Day 2 – Resentment or Reverence
Matthew 2:1-12

No sooner was Jesus born in Bethlehem than men began defining themselves by their reaction to him.

We are told that Jesus was born in the days of Herod the king. He was called Herod the Great, but he was actually a king with murder in his heart. Any king would have been worried about a new king, but Herod was doubly disturbed. He was afraid that this king would interfere with his life – his place, his power, and his plans. His reaction to the news of Jesus' birth was one of *hatred and hostility*.

There are still those who would try to destroy Jesus because his claims interfere with their lives, their plans, and their power. They wish to do what they like, and Christ comes as King to rule over them. Anyone who desires their own way never has any use for Jesus, and we feel their venom all about.

Then there were the chief priests and the scribes. When Herod wanted to know where the Christ child would be born, he went to the religious leaders of the day. They were the experts in Scripture and the law. They went around in long flowing robes. People bowed to them and called them master, and they loved the uppermost seats in the synagogue and at the banquet houses.

When the religious leaders were asked where the Messiah would be born, they didn't have to say, "Well, we'll look it up in the commentaries." They could give the answer at the drop of a hat. They knew the Scriptures and could point others to Jesus, but they would not go worship him themselves. They could recount prophecies of our Lord's birth recorded seven centuries before, and yet they were five miles from the Son of God and refused to go see him. So close, yet they missed him. Their reaction was *complete indifference*.

The religious of our Lord's day were his greatest enemies – not the harlot, not the thief, not the off-beat crowd. They were more like Herod than any would have ever thought. Their original indifference turned into hostility when confronted with the implications of Jesus' Kingship.

Today there are some like the chief priests and scribes. They can quote Scripture and know all the spiritual clichés. They know it all in their heads without knowing Christ in their heart. They are referred to as the "Triple S Saints" – they *sit*, and *soak*, and *sour*, and they give a terrible impression of Christ. All around we meet people with religion up to their ears, but without Christ in their heart. They are in church, but they aren't in Christ.

Are you in church, but not in Christ? Maybe you can quote the 23rd Psalm, the Beatitudes, the Ten Commandments, or perhaps John 3:16. You might know it all, but perhaps the Lord Jesus would say, "This people honors me with their lips, but their heart is far from me" (Matthew 15:8). It isn't what you know in your head that takes you to heaven, but *Who* you know.

Now we come into happier company. Little is known about the wise men, but we do know that they were wealthy, intelligent Gentiles who studied the stars. Their reaction to Jesus was that of *adoring worship*.

I think of these wise men as being people who had very little light. They had less light than the people in Jerusalem, because all Jerusalem knew God's promise to send the Messiah one day. The wise men had less information than Herod and less than the scribes. All they had was an awareness that God was doing something in the world. They knew this because God had given them this awareness, and they decided to seek out answers no matter how far they had to travel.

Maybe you identify with the wise men. You may know just a little, but when you heard the truth, you immediately knew that this was what you wanted. When there is true seeking, a light begins to shine until one day you fully believe, trust, and commit. You realize you've met the Lord.

Which company do you keep? Are you earnestly seeking the Lord? Are you seemingly indifferent to him or even openly hostile? Every knee will bow before the Lord Jesus one day, whether in loving awe or in dreadful fear. Answer his call to adore him as King today.

Day 3 – Whose are You?
Matthew 3:1-12

The sentry stood at his post armed and ready. His job was to see that no one passed the gate into the royal palace but those recognized by their identification with the king.

Suddenly, an elegant automobile – one of the most expensive variety – rounded the corner and screeched to a halt just outside the gates. The driver jumped from the car and opened the door for his somewhat impatient passenger. The man, obviously the object of the chauffeur's respect, rose and approached the armed guard.

"I've come to see the king," the distinguished-looking guest announced. With that, he pulled out his card and handed it to the stone-faced sentinel. No one who saw that card would question that he was an important man. He was a man of many accomplishments in the world's eyes. The guard, however, was unimpressed. "I'm sorry, sir," he curtly answered. "The king cannot see you today."

We need not repeat the industrialist's reply. The color of his face indicated his blood pressure was reaching a new high, and the words from his lips did not befit a man of such supposed dignity. He was angry to say the least.

Just about that time, an old army jeep pulled up to the gates. Out jumped a bedraggled soldier, just back from the front lines. His uniform was covered with mud and his face needed a shave. "Who goes there?" the guard questioned. Out of breath, the soldier replied, "Sir, who I am doesn't matter," and he revealed no list of accomplishments, not even a list of things done for the King in battle. He just revealed the seal of the King Himself.

Immediately, the sentry barked out, "Entrance allowed. I will announce your arrival to the King." The businessman's anger could no longer be controlled. "How dare you! I am a man of great stature in this country. I am known the world over for my accomplishments and authority. This man comes bearing none of that and no name of his own, yet he has been admitted immediately. What is the meaning of this?"

At that the guard quietly responded, "Sir, there is a war going on. The man who just passed through is assigned to the front lines representing the King. The King is not impressed with the positions of men. He is impressed only by those who come, not calling attention to *who they are, but to who he is*. Those who are about his business need no identity but that they belong to Him.

That guard could well be representing our King. We too are in the midst of an intense war and are to be known not for *who we are*, but *Who we represent*. We must remember that a world asking, "Who are you?" doesn't need to hear our name, but His. That was a fact John the Baptist understood completely, and Jesus called him great.

John the Baptist had few of the world's marks of greatness, yet in Matthew 11, Jesus called him the greatest man who had ever lived until that time – greater than Abraham, Joseph, Moses, David. John was the greatest because he was the herald of the Messiah – the One who was greater still. His job was to announce the coming of Christ and his Kingdom. His was the voice of transition from the Old Covenant to the New. Like the war-weary soldier, he was great because of Who he represented.

Day 4 – Don't Sidestep the Cross
Matthew 4

The Holy Spirit has etched into Scripture a simultaneously intense and gracious warning. I John 2:15-17 reads:

"Do not love the world or the things in the world. If anyone loves the world, the love of the Father is not in him. For all that is in the world – the desires of the flesh and the desires of the eyes and pride of possessions – is not from the Father but is from the world. And the world is passing away along with its desires, but whoever does the will of God abides forever."

Physical desires, possessions, and status are all used by the Evil One to tempt God's people. These battles started in the Garden of Eden and have continued ever since. Satan even tried to use these tactics against the Lord Jesus. God has made us whole people with legitimate physical, emotional, and spiritual needs, but sometimes Satan tempts us to satisfy a perfectly good desire in a wrong way or at the wrong time.

The first missile Satan fired in an effort to divert Jesus is found in Matthew 4:3: "And the tempter came and said to him, 'If you are the Son of God, command these stones to become loaves of bread." Jesus had not eaten for forty days, and Satan came reminding him of his very real physical needs. This wasn't a temptation for Jesus to do something bad – after all, later he multiplied the fish and the loaves. However, the primary reason for his miracles was to demonstrate spiritual truth. God is still in the miracle business, but he is sovereign and does not provide miracles on demand.

Now the temptation to turn rocks into sandwiches has not been my biggest battle, but Satan does often tempt us to meet a physical need at the expense of a spiritual one. Maybe that need is for food, or intimacy, security, or rest.

Satan also intimated in this temptation that *if you were really God's unique Son, would He care so little that He does not meet this legitimate need?* Remember that Jesus was led into the wilderness by the Holy Spirit. Was this all God's fault? Maybe God is not good, or if he is good, he doesn't have the power to provide. Has our Enemy suggested to you that if God really cared He would meet your need? Satan tries to shift the blame to God. He will do anything to take our mind off of the cross and place it on our circumstances. God has done everything necessary to restore both man and this world to what He intended.

Once you believe the lie that God deserves blame, you can be led to abandon your dependence upon God and resort to your own devices. When we begin to doubt God's Word, his goodness, or his power, we may decide: *If God is not meeting or cannot meet my needs, I'll do it myself.* This is trying to be god of your own life. What situation are you about to take over from God to meet a need your way?

Jesus did not stoop to argue either his need or his capability. He did not pretend he wasn't hungry or that he was unable to do what Satan suggested. He simply did the one thing Satan cannot tolerate – He quoted Scripture: "It is written, 'Man shall not live by bread alone, but by every word that comes from the mouth of God.'"

With missile number two, Satan again questions God's Word and also Jesus' relationship to God. He says in effect: *If what God said about you is true; prove it. Throw yourself off of the temple, and angels will rescue you.* Many Jews believed the Messiah would come in a spectacular manner from the temple, so Satan took that belief and quoted Scripture deviously.

Be very careful. Don't pull Scripture out of context, and know it well enough that others can't quote it incorrectly to mislead you. Sometimes Christians seek proof-texts to back up their own ideas instead of being honest with the Scriptures. Or some use Scripture out of context to try to twist God's arm and accomplish their own will. It is possible to back up most any idea with a text partly or wrongly used. It is true that God sends angels to guard us many times. However, do not violate a Scriptural principle, get into a position that you shouldn't, and then quote Scripture and expect God to bail you out. Don't do a work for God using wrong methods and then expect Him to bless it. Presumption is attempting to see how far we can push God for our own purposes.

Jesus would never depend on the spectacular to win people, for people are never satisfied by dramatic signs. They will always want one more. God wants people to trust him, and for those who do, He has more than proved himself at Calvary.

The third temptation was even more brash. Satan asked Jesus to make a deal with him. *Bow down to me and all the kingdoms of this world and their glory will be yours.* Satan has always wanted to be God and receive worship.

Jesus looked at all the kingdoms from the top of that mountain and knew that He had a divine right to all of them. In fact, He came for the purpose of bringing all of them under His loving rule. It was the longing of His heart, and God had promised it. BUT, God's way involved humiliation, suffering, even death. Satan offered Him a kingdom short-cut. *Here's an easier way, one without a cross.* Satan will try to help us fulfill God-given desires if we will go after them his way. He'll tell us how effective we can be as a Christian with "all these things." Why take God's way when there is a plan that is so much quicker, better, and easier?

But Satan is a liar and a counterfeit. No good deals come from Satan. His price is always immeasurably more than he leads us to believe.

This last temptation was blatant idolatry. God is a jealous God, and only he has the power and authority to fulfill our deepest longings. God jealously guards our worship because He does not want us to go through life looking everywhere but to Him for the things our heart craves. He knows we become like what we worship, and He wants us to be like Him.

We are sometimes tempted to sacrifice eternal blessing for the deceptive, disappointing, and short-lived imitations Satan offers. It is usually because God's plan for fulfilling His promises involves waiting and suffering. There was only one way for Christ to receive the eternal kingdom, and that was through the cross. This is tremendously instructive for us. So often we cry, *O God, couldn't you accomplish this some other way? I want the result, but couldn't you do it without the pain and the wait?*

Jesus met all these temptations by quoting Scripture. The devil likes to talk philosophy and even religion, and Jesus could have fought that way, but He didn't. He made no effort to defend or deliver God. He let God defend Himself. He handled the devil as we all can and must – by hitting him with Scripture.

But, you may say, *I memorized Bible verses and I quote them over and over. I am as vulnerable with my Bible as without.* There is a difference between magic and faith. Magic is trying to use an object or a chant or a Bible verse to ward off evil or to control circumstances. Faith is the quiet confidence that what God says is true enough to ACT on. Faith is believing and choosing to live by what is true.

Yes, our God will lead us into life's wilderness at times to be tested. But the very tests the devil thinks will destroy us, God uses to transform us. Then, when the enemy's onslaughts are over, God wraps His loving arms around us and sees that the pruning of the battlefield results in lasting fruit. That makes the battle worth it.

Day 5 – Empty Hands are Ready to Receive
Matthew 5:1-3

We think we are happy when our happenings happen to happen the way we want them to happen; when our outward circumstances are the way we like them. But this kind of happiness is dependent on the ups and downs of life. For many, the pursuit of happiness ends in a freakish traffic jam. Motors keep accelerating, but nobody can move. The engines are powerful, but confusion and congestion keeps them from progressing. This has caused many to forsake the pursuit altogether and wrap themselves in a cocoon of cynicism. The kind of happiness or blessedness that Jesus talks about in the Sermon on the Mount is true, permanent happiness not based on externals. It is not based on what kind of a car you drive or what brand of shoes you wear. It is not dependent on how well your children are behaving today or if the sun is shining. This happiness, or more aptly joy, is based on receiving favor from the King of Kings.

When Jesus says we will be "blessed," he means joyous, fulfilled, fortunate, to be congratulated. Joy is the result of being loved by God. When undeserved grace penetrates the thick layers of guilt and sin, there is a surge of true joy. There can be no real joy without Christ living in us. One said it well: "Joy is the standard that flies on the battlements of the heart when the King is in residence." True joy is our companion during the battle, not only after the battle.

In the Beatitudes, Jesus declares us blessed when we are characterized by eight specific things. Each one is in direct contrast to the character and conduct of this world, and each consecutive beatitude builds on the other. They are not multiple choice for us to pick and choose our favorite. You won't be able to have the last without the first. We'll cover them all over the next three days.

The first beatitude says: "Blessed are the poor in spirit, for theirs is the kingdom of heaven" (5:3). Happy are you when you realize that you are poor in spirit. This means acknowledging your abject poverty. You are not just a little short on cash until you get paid; you have nothing to offer. Jesus is speaking to those who think they have spiritual worth in their own right, saying, 'Recognize that you have *nothing*, no spiritual value that makes you acceptable on your own. You must have a humble attitude, knowing that you desperately need God.

Do you know how to catch monkeys? If you should ever need to do such a random thing, get a small can and put some peanuts in it. Then, dig a hole in the ground and imbed the can. A monkey will soon come along, sniff the peanuts, and find the little can. Then, she will stick her slim little hand down inside the small can and grab those peanuts. Now she's got a problem. With her slim little hand full of peanuts, she doesn't have a slim little hand anymore. She has a big fist. The slim hand went inside the can, but the big fist won't come out. That's how you catch monkeys.

Now you may think, 'You can't catch monkeys that way because the monkey will turn loose the nuts and pull her hand out.' But there is something you haven't reckoned with. They have a weakness for peanuts, and they are dumb. So, monkeys hang on to those peanuts and won't let go – even when the trapper comes and takes them alive. The silly thing is, that if they'd only let go of the thing that is entrapping them, they would be free!

Aren't we like that? We hang on to our funny ideas about our goodness. We keep our fist closed around self-image, self-importance, self-sufficiency. If only we would let go, confess, and reach out with an empty hand instead of a clinched fist. Do you know what God would do? God promises to give all the riches of the kingdom of heaven to those with empty hands. But it's a hard thing to be poor in spirit. It requires us to let go of our pride. It is in reaching out to the Lord, cognizant of our empty hands, that our pride is snuffed out and our joy is kindled.

Day 6 – Upside Down Blessing
Matthew 5:4-7

"Blessed are those who mourn, for they shall be comforted" (Matthew 5:4). The mourners are those who are broken-hearted over their sin. Someone might readily admit: "I'm poor and weak, not doing the things I should, hanging on to what I shouldn't. My hand is a clenched fist, not open to God." You can say these things, agreeing that life isn't what it should be, all without mourning about it. This is a sign of a hard heart. Jesus said to admit to the poverty of your spirit, and instead of saying, "Well, that's just how it is," mourn over it. Then you'll be blessed. Do not rationalize sin. See how broken-hearted God is over it. Recognize that Jesus Christ had to die on account of your sin and mine, and then your heart will properly mourn.

The good news is that a state of mourning is not your final destination! God says that when you come to the point of being poor in spirit and mourn about your sin, you will be comforted. One of the wonderful titles Jesus gave to the Holy Spirit is that of Comforter. That doesn't mean that he will pat you on the hand and say, "That's alright. Never mind about that." But he does remind the mourning heart of the wonderful grace of Jesus that is truly greater than all of our sin.

Verse 5 says: "Blessed are the meek, for they shall inherit the earth." The good news is that meek is not the same thing as weak or pathetic, as some might suppose. Whereas weakness is yielding to the old sinful nature, meekness is being yielded to God - yielded to His Word and to His will as expressed in our circumstances. One has said that it is yielding our self-will to God and giving up ill-will toward others. Meekness is tied to being humbly receptive toward God and gentle toward other people. Meekness is strength under control, but it is not my strength or my control. Jesus says that he is meek and lowly of heart. It is of his meekness that we partake.

Now we come to the fourth beatitude, verse six: "Blessed are those who hunger and thirst for righteousness, for they shall be satisfied."

Do you know what it is to have righteousness? As a child I thought it was to sport a pious look, smile all the time, never fly off the handle even when you hit your thumb with a hammer. But that is not correct. It literally means: right-standing before God in terms of position and condition.

Before I knew Jesus Christ, I was in wrong-standing with God, but because of his blood, I am made righteous. I can walk into His Presence any time, without any condemnation. As a result, I am told to long to incorporate that right-standing into my practice, to yearn for my life to display the righteousness of

Christ that is graciously mine. It is a process. I find every day, every week, new areas in my life that I need to bring into right-standing before God.

Unfortunately, we can get the impression that our hunger for righteousness is forever satiated by praying a prayer for salvation. Our sins are forgiven, we are going to heaven, and righteousness doesn't really concern the present. If I do something bad, I'll just say 'I'm sorry,' and Jesus will forgive me. If he tells me to do something I don't want to do, I'll just say no, and he'll forgive me. Taking Jesus as my Savior really doesn't have to change my life very much.

Picture a scene that illustrates how absurd this is: The wedding is over; the cake has been cut. As the limo pulls away from the well-wishers, suppose the bride scoots away from her groom and says, "Please take me home."

He looks at her in astonishment. "But you know our house won't be ready for a couple more weeks. The heat and water aren't connected yet."

"Oh," she says, "I don't mean YOUR home. Take me back to my mother. Look, now that we're married, I'll try to see you once a week if it's convenient, but I'm going back to my old way of life. Of course I love you. I've accepted you as my husband, haven't I? We just settled all that, but don't think that is going to change the way I live. Now, if I get sick, or need more money, or if something comes up I can't handle, I'll call you right away. I'll expect you to take care of things, because you are my husband. In the meantime, thank you for loving me, making me yours, but hands off my life until I'm old and have had my fun."

That would not be a marriage; that would be a mockery. Yet, that is the way thousands of professing believers treat the Lord Jesus. They say by their lives, if not with their lips: "Lord, I have accepted you as my Savior. Thank you for saving me, for preparing Heaven. Someday I want to be with you, but now I have my own interests to consider. I'll try to see you once a week on Sunday, but I have my place at the beach, my boat, and my career to think of. However, now that I'm yours, I expect you to answer my prayers. If I'm sick, if I lose my job, or things get beyond me, I'll expect you to come running. But in the meantime, I really don't want to be bothered by spending time with you, or thinking about what you want from me." There is no hunger or thirst for a real relationship. On the contrary, our secure position in Christ must stir up a hunger and thirst for more of him.

Verse seven says, "Blessed are the merciful, for they shall receive mercy." The natural by-product of being filled with God's Spirit is being merciful to others. This is one of the first things we should see in one who has recognized where she would be without Jesus. She is so overwhelmed by the mercy poured out on her by Christ that she cannot but be merciful to those around her. The only way you can be merciful is to recognize that you are poor in spirit – that you would be utterly lost apart from Jesus. Only then are you able to see another's situation with His eyes of compassion.

These prescriptions for God's blessing are quite upside-down in the eyes of the world, but you can't imagine the beauty of the view from his perspective. You just might find that you are seeing right-side-up for the first time.

Day 7 – The Blessing of Reproach
Matthew 5:8-12

"Blessed are the pure in heart, for they shall see God" (Matthew 5:8). Pure means wholly unmixed. We cannot serve two masters. A pure heart is set only on God and his Kingdom; it has a singleness of purpose. The blessed result of a heart set on the Lord alone is that you will indeed see him. The pure in heart do not strain their eyes in vain to see the Lord; Jesus promises that their eyes will feast upon him.

The next beatitude reads: "Blessed are the peacemakers, for they shall be called sons of God" (verse 9). Peace has been made for those who look to Christ for salvation. D.L. Moody said, "Many people are trying to make peace, but that has already been done at Calvary. All we have to do is enter into it." Our peace is the result of Christ's finished work on the cross, and it only grows as He lives his life in us through the Holy Spirit. This is spiritual peace between God and man. As a result of the spiritual peace that He has wrought in us, we can reveal the Prince of Peace to a world that often unknowingly cries out for Jesus. Jesus reconciles us with the Father, and we are to be reconciled to one another. When we receive the peace he offers, we too can become peacemakers.

A heart in line with the beatitudes results in the Lord's gracious favor, but you will quickly find yourself at odds with the world. Jesus is very honest about this. Verses 10-12 say: "Blessed are those who are persecuted for righteousness' sake, for theirs is the kingdom of heaven. Blessed are you when others revile you and persecute you and utter all kinds of evil against you falsely on my account. Rejoice and be glad, for your reward is great in heaven, for so they persecuted the prophets who were before you." We might call this the blessing nobody initially wants.

Please don't listen to those who say, "Come to Jesus, and all your problems will be over." Jesus himself says that when we start living for him, we will have persecution and antagonism. Yet, even then, we are blessed.

In the midst of persecution, never feel guilty for thinking of God's promised reward and keeping your eye on the heavenly prize. Jesus did. Hebrews tells us that Jesus endured the cross and its shame because of the joy set before him. Moses tossed aside the wealth of Egypt to bear the reproach of being an Israelite, because he had his eyes on the reward. They had the ability to stand on their convictions without compromising. They were willing to accept the consequences by fixing their eyes on what God is preparing for those who love him.

In the Beatitudes, Jesus explained that true happiness comes when we submit to his Lordship and receive his approval. See your need. Mourn your sin.

Submit to your King. Hunger for a life pleasing to him, extend the mercy he has shown you, and keep your eyes and heart centered on his Kingdom. Show the world the peace that your King offers, and don't be surprised when others don't want to hear that there is a King besides themselves. It is then that you will be truly blessed.

Day 8 – Righteousness Redefined
Matthew 5:17-48

"For I tell you, unless your righteousness exceeds that of the scribes and Pharisees, you will never enter the kingdom of heaven." - Matthew 5:20

What a bombshell! Jesus' listeners were stunned. They looked at each other with amazement – *How can we be more righteous than our leaders?* This is perhaps the key to the whole of the Sermon on the Mount.

The "righteousness" of the religious leaders was based on self-effort, which Jesus and all of Scripture contradicted. The Bible opposes little more vehemently than the religion of human achievement. The sort of righteousness exemplified by the Pharisees was not sufficient to gain entrance into his Kingdom, because they did not live up to the standards of God. They did not possess true internal righteousness, that which comes from Christ alone.

Self-righteousness differs from God's righteousness in several important ways. It is external, partial, redefined, self-centered, and insufficient!

The righteousness of God is genuine inner righteousness, which God has always prized. When Samuel was ready to anoint Jesse's oldest son, the Lord said: "Do not look at his appearance because I have rejected him…God sees not as man sees, for man looks at the outward appearance but the Lord looks at the heart."

We receive Christ's righteousness when we are saved, and this is what gives us right-standing with God. Christ then changes us from the inside out. Because of Christ's righteousness graced to us and the power of the Holy Spirit living in us, this genuine righteousness produces external fruit. It is not as though genuine righteousness is hidden away in the heart and therefore invisible. When we are gradually transformed into the likeness of the Lord, our righteousness becomes increasingly visible. The Pharisees' problem was not that their righteousness was visible, it was that it was *only* visible – merely skin deep. Their hearts had not been made new.

Jesus goes on to teach about what it really means not to murder or commit adultery, pinpointing the heart issues that lead to those actions and calling the sin in the heart the deed itself. This probably discouraged some in the crowd, knowing that it was impossible for them to refrain from anger or lust completely. This was the point. On our own, we cannot walk righteously, nor even desire to! The righteous requirements of the heart can only be met as a result of the blood of our Savior shed for us. Our hearts are so evil that we must have a heart transplant. God is not in the business of fixing hearts; He replaces them.

Jesus spends a large portion of the Sermon on the Mount dismantling attitudes of self-sufficiency and paving the way for the poor in spirit to see him as their only hope. Their *only* hope, yes, but a *sure* hope indeed.

Day 9 – To God be the Glory
Matthew 6

An old preacher once observed that the greatest danger to Christianity is that the old self simply becomes religious. The hypocrites of whom Jesus speaks in Matthew 6 had convinced themselves that they became acceptable to God by performing certain religious acts, including giving, praying, and fasting. People still deceive themselves into thinking that they are Christians, when all they have done is dress their old nature in religious garments.

In Matthew 5, our Lord explained what we are to *be* –perfect as our Heavenly Father is perfect. Now he will tell us *how* He wants us to live out that perfection. Matthew 6:1 says, "Beware of practicing your righteousness before other people in order to be seen by them, for then you will have no reward from your Father who is in heaven."

In this passage, *reward* is a key word. It is mentioned seven times. God promises a reward to those who do their good works unto him (verse 4), and it is not unspiritual to think about the reward or desire this reward. God's reward doesn't leave us empty and disappointed like an old trophy; it is truly satisfying. The apostle Paul knew about that reward, and he tells us that he pressed toward the goal with every fiber of his being. God has set a splendid prize before you, provided you are running as unto him. Those who stop to flex their muscles for the crowd forfeit the reward. Do not sound trumpets to call attention to your giving or wear a gloomy face when you are fasting.

Are you seeking to please God or men? It is so tempting to live to impress others, for our flesh loves praise and recognition. Called to live a life unto God, believers realistically have to live that life before men. With the human heart desperately wicked and deceitful, this is a tricky business. The devil knows all about our egos and how much self craves recognition, and he puts pressure on us to seek the approval of men. He suggests that the praise from an unseen God is nowhere near as satisfying as praise from flesh and blood.

Though we are not to do good works before men *in order* to be seen, Jesus said that our works nevertheless must be seen. "In the same way, let your light shine before others, so that they may see your good works and give glory to your Father who is in heaven" (Matthew 5:16). The question is not whether or not our good works should be seen by others, but whether or not they are done to that end. May the psalmist's prayer be ours: "Not to us, O Lord, not to us, but to your name give glory, for the sake of your steadfast love and faithfulness" (Psalm 115:1)!

Day 10 – Construction versus Demolition
Matthew 7:1-5

"Judge not, that you be not judged. For with the judgment you pronounce you will be judged, and with the measure you use, it will be measured to you." - Matthew 7:1-2

What did Jesus mean – "Judge not"? Our culture has erased the line between the type of judging that Jesus is talking about and the wise practice of discerning. It is imperative that we understand the difference. We must distinguish between judgmental slander and loving admonishment. One is disobedience and the other is clearly obedience.

In these verses, "judge" doesn't mean evaluate, but it means to condemn. There is a great chasm between evaluating (which we are to do) and condemning (which we are not to do). In the context of this chapter, Jesus teaches that some judgment and criticism is sinful, but some critical abilities are commended and even commanded. Jesus is not speaking here about calling sin what it is. He is speaking of our motive and the way we go about it. Some people are critical of everything. Others never criticize, never evaluate or discern anything. They are so tolerant that everything is acceptable. Both are foolish.

The challenge of a Christian is to discover how to exercise God-given critical abilities in a way that glorifies him and aims to restore others.

Jesus, the Master Teacher, uses some humor to teach us how to do this. In verses 3-5 Jesus says that we are not to pick sawdust from another's eye when there is a plank of wood in our own. How can you see through your plank to remove their sawdust? Take the plank from your own eye, and then you can see clearly to remove the speck from your brother's eye.

There is something about us that makes us want to rush to help others before we begin to recognize or address our own problems. Jesus says that Christians are to be loving speck-removers, but first we must check ourselves for planks. We can become so concerned about what is wrong with somebody else – everybody else – that we don't discover the glaringly obvious sin in ourselves.

It takes humility to be willing to do something about the problem in your own life, and Jesus requires us to do some humble self-examination. If we expended half the energy examining ourselves that we do examining others, we would have enough lumber to start a lumberyard.

What are some common logs that prevent us from seeing clearly, from building up the body of Christ in a helpful way? If we look inside, we might find jealousy, stubbornness, or a spirit of superiority. When the Spirit graciously illuminates the plank in your eye, don't just say, *Well, here I am with my plank. I've always had it. Mother had it. It's a family trait.* Ask God to help you remove it, and in faith draw upon the Holy Spirit's power to walk in obedience.

After we have taken care of our own sins, then Christ expects us to help others. But this still does not permit us to have a spirit of criticism or arrogance that leads us to assume we have a right to judge others' hearts. There is one and only one Judge – Jesus Christ, appointed by the Father. He has all the facts. He is impartial. He is merciful, and he is just. He is unaffected by circumstantial evidence, and he has the supreme qualification: He is able to look upon the heart.

Jesus will tell us later in this sermon that we should make judgments about the *fruit* others bear, but we are commanded not to ever condemn another Christian. Jesus says sawdust removal is appropriate, but it is a ministry of *love*. When we are called upon to correct others, we should be like a good doctor whose purpose is to bring healing, not like an enemy who destroys.

If you are all around critical of a person, it is not your ministry to pull out their speck. Attend to the plank in your own eye. The worst kind of critical is hypocritical. It operates on the devil's standard. It has the remarkable ability to condone in oneself the identical things you condemn in others, or even to condone far worse in yourself. If you just don't like a person, you are probably not the one to tell them about the speck in their eye. Love is concerned with the wellbeing of the other person. Speck removal is a constructive ministry.

Day 11 – Broken Down Barriers
Matthew 8:1-4

After Jesus' sermon in chapters 5-7, his disciples followed him down the side of the mountain and back into the real world. Jesus' feet had barely touched the soil at the foot of the mountain before large crowds arrived with real and messy problems.

The first to approach him was a leper. This would have been an easy confrontation to avoid. The man was an untouchable. But Jesus had come to seek and save those who knew they were lost, and this man knew. Not only was his body marred, but his spirit was broken. No one dared touch him, befriend him, or love him, because he had been declared "unclean". The man full of leprosy and destined for death had no hope till he came to Jesus.

How wonderful that our God is approachable in Jesus! Though fully God incarnate, Jesus was an approachable man. We have a wonderfully approachable God, but we also want to come with the right attitude, as this man did. He *knelt* before him. Outwardly, his appearance was loathsome and repulsive, but inwardly he was reverent and believing. By contrast, the scribes and Pharisees were doubtless richly attired, yet they were inwardly proud and unbelieving. They were filled with a far more deadly leprosy of the heart.

The leper came to Jesus with humility and expectant faith. He didn't come demanding or claiming to deserve healing. He did, however, acknowledge Jesus' ability to heal him, uttering these memorable words: "Lord, if you will, you can make me clean." Don't you love it? *Lord, I don't know if it's your will or not, but I know one thing – It's well within your power.* The man knew that Jesus was not obligated to heal him and yet perfectly capable of doing so. He left his situation in the Lord's hands.

This leper shows us how to come to Jesus. He came *acknowledging his need* and with *reverent worship*. He came *boldly*, because he believed Jesus was approachable and with *faith*, because he believed Jesus was compassionate and had the power to heal him.

Something supernatural happened that day. This uncomely leper who had nothing in which to boast saw Jesus as his only hope. He reached out in faith, and Jesus reached out his hand and touched him.

Don't you love verse three? "And Jesus stretched out his hand and touched him, saying, 'I will; be clean.'" Immediately the man was cured. He became whole, completely restored – all because Jesus put out his hand and touched him. The Son of God lovingly touches the outcast, those others would not even come near.

This is a physical sign representing a spiritual truth. Leprosy is a picture of our sinful condition. Imagine Jesus, the holy and pure God, touching you and I in our defilement. He has not only touched us, but picked us up and embraced us. The Bible says that he was made sin for us. Jesus embraced my defilement and imparted to me his wholeness.

Have you come with the reverent attitude of that leper and specifically asked for Jesus' cleansing? He is the only one who can make you whole and clean. If you don't bring your sin to Jesus, it will fester until one day you will realize that it has destroyed you. Like the leper, recognize that apart from God's supernatural touch, there is no hope, no help, no life. We must fall down before Jesus and cry out: *Lord, I need to be healed from the disease of sin. I know you are willing because you died to take it away.* Then, he will whisper to you, *Be cleansed.* He'll reach out and touch you if only you'll ask him in faith and humility. There is something very appropriate about the fact that the first miracle Matthew records is the cleansing of the leper. The purest One to ever walk the earth willingly touched a leper. It is beautifully crazy, and so is the love of God toward sinners.

Day 12 – Not Guilty by Association
Matthew 9:9-13

The brand-new convert opened his house to all of his old friends and invited Jesus, the One who had changed his life, to fellowship with them.

Jesus accepted Matthew's invitation gladly. He wanted to be with liars, extortionists, and thieves so that he could save those who were lost. He was in the most logical place for God to be in a sinful and dying world – where dying sinners were.

The religious leaders were hesitant to directly criticize Jesus, so they began to question his disciples instead. "Why does your teacher eat with tax collectors and sinners?" You can see "Ronny Righteous" call Peter aside and ask: "What gives here? If you guys are so spiritual, why are you sitting down with the scum of the earth? Naughty, naughty." The religious crowd didn't take too well to what was going on. This man was eating and drinking with outcasts! That didn't fit their concept of God at all; therefore, this man couldn't be God.

They might have addressed the disciples, but they had to deal with their Master anyway. Jesus didn't ignore them; nor did he apologize for being himself. He simply explained the truth. Don't you love his response? *I am the Great Physician. It is not the healthy who need a doctor, but the sick. I have not come to listen to sick people tell me how well they are. I have come to help people who know they are sick and are willing to admit it.*

Then he told the Pharisees to do some homework and sent them to the Old Testament to discover the Lord values. Verse thirteen says, "Go and learn what this means: 'I desire mercy, not sacrifice.'" Many years before, the prophet Hosea pointed out that God was not interested in mere religious observance, but in mercy toward others.

Then, Jesus looked those religious hypocrites straight in the eye and uttered these words: "I have not come to call the righteous, but sinners." Not the self-righteous, but those who know they are sinners. Jesus is here today to heal you of the very things that you wish you didn't have. He came for those who have needs and will admit it. No one who will come is beyond his help. No life is too sick for his touch to restore and redeem. The only ones he does not help are those who refuse to acknowledge him and receive his cure.

Those scribes were afraid to rub shoulders with sinners, for fear their goodness would be lost. But the publicans, because they sensed their need, were able to rub shoulders with the Savior. The scribes thought they were impressively healthy; they never considered that they needed a doctor. The publicans were simply waiting for the Doctor to arrive.

We might ask: If people need Jesus so badly, why don't they come to our churches? Maybe its because they haven't been invited to our party. They need someone to get to know them, to love them. Are we a bunch of doctors who refuse to make house calls? Is it that we would rather sit around the hospital and treat each other than go out into the highways and byways where people are dying to give them the prescription for life?

Jesus wants us to respond to the invitations of people in the world so we can demonstrate the difference between light and darkness and be his salt in a dying world. He would accept that invitation to the dinner party. Jesus in you wants to go there, and people will be changed because you and HE went. He left heaven and came to where we are, so we can eventually be where he is. But until then, host dinner parties and barbeques and eat with those who need the Master.

Go home today and answer the phone. It may be Matthew inviting you to a banquet. Go. Then it may ring tomorrow, too. That may be a scribe taunting you for going. Let him. Jesus Christ in you has a job to do. He has come to seek and save the lost. He would go wherever they are. Let him.

Incidentally, there will be another feast coming that will top any that we have gone to. It too will be filled with people that some of us didn't think would be invited. If it weren't glory, we might wonder why Jesus was fellowshipping with the likes of them. They might wonder that about us.

Day 13 – To Fear or Not to Fear
Matthew 10:16-31

Jesus never minced words. The Lord gave clear warning about the reception the world would give his disciples. Identifying with Christ propelled them headfirst into intense cosmic conflict, into the battle between Satan and God. That battle is still raging. As the Holy Spirit speaks through us, we will be witnesses to those who would persecute us – government officials, sometimes even religious groups, or members of our own family. Some governments outright forbid the proclamation of the gospel and persecute witnesses; others are more subtle. Religious groups persecute genuine believers as well. Almost any religion in America is protected, except Christianity. Some so-called churches and religious groups alienate or endanger those who stand up for the truth of God's Word. As Christ's followers today, we must also be prepared for persecution to come from our own families. Family members are either drawn to Christianity or they are repelled by it. Families can be broken on the Rock that is Christ. He talks specifically about this in 10:35-37.

Despite this hard news, we can take comfort in the fact that Jesus makes provision for His followers who are persecuted (v.19-20). He promises that God's Spirit will speak through us when we don't know what to say. He will equip us to be victorious no matter the circumstances. Still, we must make a choice to stand with God or yield to the pressures of persecution. Jesus' instruction is to endure to the end (v.22), and the apostle Paul wrote that for those who endure there awaits an eternal weight of glory beyond all comparison. Now, endurance does not produce salvation, rather it is evidence of it. Where there is a genuine work of God, there will be perseverance. In this, we find great comfort.

There are two things that we naturally fear: what people will say and what they will do. Jesus gives the antidote to both fears. Do not be afraid of men, he says, for one day all that is hidden will be revealed. On Judgment Day, everyone will know the truth about Christ. In the meantime, proclaim it. "What I tell you in the dark, say in the light, and what you hear whispered, proclaim on the housetops" (v.27). Physical death might be the price for speaking God's truth. But the death of the body does not result in the death of the soul. The faithful disciple values her soul immeasurably more than she values her body and will gladly sacrifice that which is corruptible for that which is incorruptible. Besides all that, someone once said: "God's servants are immortal until their work is done."

Jesus says to focus your fear of men in another direction. Look ahead to the day when you will stand before God. That will deal with the fears of the "they" out there. If we fear God, we need fear nothing else.

26

Now, lest we misunderstand the fear of God, Jesus reminds us of God's tender love. This is one of the most beautiful, comforting pictures ever given by God. "Are not two sparrows sold for a penny? And not one of them will fall to the ground apart from your Father. But even the hairs of your head are all numbered. Fear not, therefore; you are of more value than many sparrows" (Matthew 10:29-31). That's the kind of God we serve – One whose care extends to the minutest detail of our lives. That is the God Jesus wants us to fear. If you understand God's great and tender love for you, then you will be fearless when confronted by those that may try to harm the body. When you go out into the world and the enemy threatens and your heart begins to sink, remember: *I am loved by the God who knows the number of hairs on my head, and one day I will stand before this God to give account. He is one I am to fear.*

Day 14 – Relaying Hope
Matthew 11:2-6

"Now when John heard in prison about the deeds of Christ, he sent word by his disciples and said to him, 'Are you the one who is to come, or shall we look for another?'" – Matthew 11:2

We don't know what kind of doubts had entered the mind of John or what exactly prompted the question he conveyed to Jesus. We do know that John was in prison because he was faithful to reprove Herod for his wickedness, and he had been in prison for about a year. His day of popularity was over. Humanly speaking, the career of John the Baptist had ended in disaster. The fiery and courageous man was bound and bruised. Things had surely changed since the days of his baptisms in the Jordan. We can understand, that having come to a place like that, John might have doubts and questions. When we are suffering, oftentimes doubts are allowed to fester.

Why would I, the King's herald, the one sent to proclaim the Lamb of God, end up in a dank prison? And this while Herod lives on in power and seeming success. Why, if Jesus is the Messiah, does he appear to care so little and do nothing?

Jesus did not seem to be bringing an axe to the root of the tree. His ministry bore little resemblance to the ministry of judgment John had foretold. He was a different sort of Messiah from what John had imagined. He, like most of the Jews of Jesus' time, didn't realize that the Messiah had to suffer. They accepted the part about Jesus coming to earth and ruling from Jerusalem – but the part about his rejection, suffering, and carrying their sins went right over their heads. Not even John expected a Servant King.

However, John was an honest doubter. He was not questioning the truthfulness of God's Word; he was just uncertain about his understanding of those truths. This kind of doubting and questioning can occur in the life of any believer.

Believers today are often confused about God for the same reasons. We have our own ideas of how God should do things. We read the Bible, and a text seems to leap off the page. We've taken it completely out of context, and yet we build our life on it because it says what we want it to say. When God doesn't fit our preconceived ideas of what he should be like, we are perplexed.

When a believer has faithfully and sacrificially served the Lord for many years and then experiences tragedy, perhaps a series of tragedies, it is difficult not to wonder about God's love and justice. We are tempted to ask, *God where are you when I really need you?* Difficult circumstances can cause us to have honest questions and doubt.

Should we hesitate to ask them because we are supposed to have all the answers? Satan loves it when we are afraid to ask the questions that can lead to deeper understanding. We may hate to ask because our questions reveal our need and make us feel vulnerable. They may expose gaping holes in our personality, theology, or lifestyle. Questions that are aired force an honesty that we are often unwilling to confront, so we allow our doubts to fester.

Wisely, John did not stuff his questions. He sent his disciples to Jesus. This should be our response to doubts and questions as well. Go to the Lord himself and ask him to quell your doubts, fears, and anxieties. Faith does not stop short of approaching God and praying, *Lord, I believe. Help my unbelief.*

This passage reveals something about how Jesus reacts to our moments of honest weakness and doubt. He could have just sent John a brief answer, saying: "Yes, I am Messiah." Instead, Jesus sent the disciples back to tell John, "The blind receive their sight and the lame walk, lepers are cleansed and the deaf hear, and the dead are raised up, and the poor have good news preached to them." Jesus sent John a word from the Word (see Isaiah 29, 35, and 61), saying in essence: *These are the things I am doing. Look at your Bible and see if what I am doing and what the Word says about the Messiah are congruent.*

When calamity comes and I ask questions, Jesus normally sends me back to Scripture. Go to the Bible with your questions, but don't just make the text say what you want to hear. Be open to really hearing what God says. Jesus used the Word of God and his works to authenticate his Person. Although Jesus did nothing to relieve John's circumstances, he relieved his doubts by confirming that He was indeed the long-awaited Messiah.

Jesus doesn't always change our circumstances either, but he will send his Word of comfort and assurance that he is God and his Word is sure. The Word of God and the works of God in our life are encouragement in times of doubt and discouragement.

Everyone has doubts sometimes. The question is whether your questions will stand between you and God or whether they will press you closer to him. I believe God prefers his children to come and cry: *God, this makes no sense to me. I hurt so badly. I just don't understand. But God, I love you and trust you and rest in the fact that you know how I feel. You've been here. You've been rejected by those you created and had your body broken on the cross. I can't understand what is happening to me, but help me to glorify you through it all.*

Day 15 – Mercy, Not Sacrifice
Matthew 12:1-13

The battle was over the Sabbath – a sacred day in Israel. The Sabbath was a blessing that God had given his people. It was also one of the things that made Israel unique. Every six days they stopped work and spent an entire day focused on their God.

Sabbath rest was a picture God had given to teach man the priority of God and to draw attention to the fact that man was not to live on bread alone. It was also to draw attention to the coming of the Son of God, who would take our burdens and give us rest. The Sabbath was never designed to make life more difficult, but rather to make it more meaningful. But, if man takes the principles of God and turns them into a religious system, it is only a short time until the truths are no longer visible and there is only restricting legalism.

By Jesus' day, the Sabbath had been so adulterated by the Jewish leaders that the original principle was lost. Through the years, the leaders had turned the Sabbath into a maze of meaningless regulations. What was intended by God for his glory and the good of man turned into little more than tradition. The Sabbath was not only *not* God-glorifying – it had become a stumbling block and a great burden to the people. That may be why Matthew inserted this story just after Jesus invited the burdened and heavy-laden to come to him for rest.

By Jesus' day, religious leaders had classified "work" into 39 different categories. Four of those included reaping, winnowing, threshing, and preparing a meal. So, in this section of Matthew, the disciples technically broke four rules. Verse one reads: "At that time Jesus went through the grainfields on the Sabbath. His disciples were hungry, and they began to pluck heads of grain and to eat." The offense was not stealing. According to Exodus 23 and Deuteronomy 23, they had permission to eat from the stalks that grew by the way. The accusation was that it had been done on the Sabbath. To the Pharisees, this was a grievous offense. To Jesus, their grief illuminated the fact that a beautiful gift had been made into a horrendous idol.

As always, Jesus held their petty arguments up to the light of Scripture, and their arguments dissolved into nothing. He spoke to them of their beloved King David, illustrating from I Samuel 21 how it was permissible for a ceremonial regulation to be violated to meet the legitimate needs of God's people. He asked them if they were familiar enough with the law to know that even the priests break some of their Sabbath rules. And finally he asked, "Don't you know that God desires mercy and not sacrifice?" In other words, "Don't you teachers of Scripture understand what it says?"

Jesus then blew the religious leaders out of the water with two statements about his deity. "I tell you that one greater than the temple is here" (v.6). And, "The Son of Man is Lord of the Sabbath" (v.8). Everything in the temple was arranged according to the Word of God and pointed to Jesus and his redemptive work. Claiming to be Lord of the Sabbath put him on par with God. Jesus had just told the people that he had come to give rest (chapter 11), and now he says, "I am the Lord of God's rest." The claim was clear, and the Pharisees could not walk away from that. So, they decided to use a needy man to trap Jesus.

"He went on from there and entered their synagogue. And a man was there with a withered hand. And they asked him, 'Is it lawful to heal on the Sabbath?' – so that they might accuse him" (v.9). Jesus turned to his attackers and deliberately confronted their petrified Sabbath rules. He asked, "Which one of you who has a sheep, if it falls into a pit on the Sabbath, will not take hold of it and lift it out" (v.11)? Again, they could make no reply, so he said: "So it is lawful to do good on the Sabbath" (v. 12).

Jesus commanded the man to stretch out his hand, and the hand that was long-shriveled opened in wholeness and health. Thus, Jesus' act embodied the wholeness that the Sabbath was intended to bring. At the same time, he exposed the wasted hands of the Pharisees – hands bound by their warmed-over piety, hands crippled by stinginess, hands withered by their legalism and their arrogance. In their self-righteousness, they had lost the concern for others that characterizes God. In fact, their religious legalism led them to become ungodly. Those men were concerned over their rules but cared nothing for the man's suffering. They wanted to use his hurt to attack Jesus. In contrast, Jesus cared about the man and willingly faced criticism to help him. You and I are much closer to Jesus when we are meeting others' needs than when we try to force others to live up to our manmade standards.

Day 16 – Tilled Ground
Matthew 13:18-23

Sitting down beside the sea, Jesus told the great crowd a parable about a farmer. The man went out to sow seed, and the seed landed on four different types of soil – most of which were unreceptive to the seed and one that was receptive and ultimately fruitful. Jesus then began to explain this parable in detail. This story helps us see some of the reasons why there are different reactions to the Word of God.

Verse 19 says: "When anyone hears the word of the kingdom and does not understand it, the evil one comes and snatches away what has been sown in his heart. This is what was sown along the path."

The seed is the Word of God, the message of the kingdom. It is a seed that has life in it. The seed might be a simple Christian testimony, a sermon, or just a word dropped into a conversation that will take root and change a life. Though the seed may seem small and insignificant, it is a powerful seed, for it is through this seed that the Spirit of God brings forth faith.

The focus of the parable, however, is not on the seed as much as the soil into which the seed is dropped. The soil represents the human heart, and when the seed and the soil get together, there is potential for fruit. The variable is the fertility of the soil.

The first heart is hard like a beaten path, and when the Word comes, the evil one (represented by the birds in the parable) snatches the seed away. The problem is not with the seed, but with the soil.

The second heart is shallow soil. The soil of Palestine lies on a thick layer of limestone, so few roots can go very deep. As a result, the plant springs up quickly but withers when the root system cannot sustain it. This type of soil is someone who flits from this to that, one experience to another, never content with anything for long. They may be enthusiastic for the gospel this week and a witness for vitamin supplements the next. These people live on the surface of waves of emotion. They receive the gospel gladly, but when the seasons change and troubles come, they immediately wither and die. The devil took care of the first heart; the flesh takes care of this one.

The third heart describes the typical American. The trouble in this case is not disinterest or shallowness, but rather a desire to have it all. It is not enough for the gardener to love flowers. He must also hate weeds. This soil had weeds representing the world's influences that choked and crowded out the seed and kept it from bearing fruit. The world engages us in busyness and in trying to amass riches. It calls us to center our attention on things instead of people, material wealth instead of spiritual growth. The world is also at work to keep us unfruitful.

The wise woman asks herself a series of questions as Jesus' explanation progresses: *Has the Word bounced off of me like seed off of a hard road? Has it begun to grow in me so that I can face pressures and criticism? What concerns me more than growing in God's Word?*

Finally, we see the fourth soil – the good soil. This is a heart that also receives the Word gladly, but in this case, the work continues. As she ponders over it and obeys it, the seed grows and bears much fruit – thirty, sixty, or a hundred fold! This woman receives the Word and holds fast to what she has received.

The main question the parable poses is: *What is your response to God's Word? Primarily, what is your response to Jesus, who is the very Word of God?*

It is important to remember that our Lord is not saying that once rocky soil, always rocky soil. He is not saying that hearts are unchangeable. A heart may be hard, shallow, or crowded, but the Holy Spirit changes hearts. If your heart is in an unsatisfactory condition today, He is able to till it. We know hearts can be changed by God's grace. In fact, that is the only way they can be changed.

Once our hearts have been softened to God's Word by the Holy Spirit, we must not neglect to guard them (Proverbs 4:23). Hebrews 4:14 warns believers not to become hardhearted and resistant to God's Word. Plead with the Lord to keep your heart soft, and by all means, join the sowers!

Day 17 – Loud Worship, Cold Hearts
Matthew 15:3-6

"And why do you break the commandment of God for the sake of your tradition? For God commanded, 'Honor your father and your mother,' and 'Whoever reviles father or mother must surely die.' But you say, 'If anyone tells his father or his mother, "What you would have gained from me is given to God," he need not honor his father.' So for the sake of your tradition you have made void the word of God." - Matthew 15:3-6

The Pharisees knew God's commandments backwards and forwards. They could easily recite the fifth one – "Honor your father and mother", but they nevertheless found a pious way to disobey it.

The rabbis had developed a system that allowed a person to call all of his possessions "corban." Such possessions were not to be used for anything but service to God, and if for example, their parents needed financial assistance, he or she would say: *Anything I might have used to help you has been given to God.* At the same time, those possessions could remain in the owner's hands, and if he decided to use them for his own purposes, he would simply say corban over them again. It was a hypocritical way of replacing God's specific command to honor your parents with a contradictory tradition. The religious leaders of the day had emptied God's command of its intention and substituted their traditions. They used religion to mask their disobedient hearts.

God plainly commands us to honor our parents, and that means giving them support if they need it. This was a command given with a promise for those who are obedient and a warning for those who are not. Perhaps you feel your parents are not worthy of honor. Even so, God will help you obey his commands.

Obedience to God's Word – not adherence to human tradition – is the mark of authentic spirituality. It is amazing how we can try to escape a responsibility in a pious way. We know what God has said, but we work hard at rationalizing it away. It is easy to spot this tendency in our children. They know what we said and what we meant, but they try to get around it. We are not really so different. We use religious activity to excuse our selfish desires. We find a loophole that allows us to avoid tough obedience. We can be over-zealous for tradition while neglecting the truth it represents or the One to whom it points.

Jesus was pointed and fearless in his response to the Pharisees. They were play-acting religion, and he called them hypocrites. He told them that inner purity, not external ceremony is what matters to God. He told them that Isaiah was right in prophesying about them: "This people honors me with their lips, but their heart is far from me; in vain do they worship me, teaching as doctrines the commandments of men" (v.8-9). These are God's words of judgment on people guilty of loud worship and cold hearts.

Tradition makes it easy to honor God with the lips while the heart harbors ungodliness. With David, we need to pray: *Create in me a clean heart, O God.* Rationalization cloaked as religion is dangerous, causing us to lose touch with what God's Word really teaches. We look pristine, but our hearts cannot stand up under God's examination. We need to stop looking at what we do or don't do.

Ask God to examine you and give you a heart that longs to love and obey him. When your heart is right, your behavior will follow. Ask yourself: *How have I rationalized a plain word of Scripture in order to do what I want to do?* Confess it to the Lord and walk in the obedience that flows from an undivided heart.

Day 18 – The Gift of Faith
Matthew 16:13-20

Jesus had been teaching and re-teaching, demonstrating and re-demonstrating the truth about who he was for two-and-a-half years. Now only six months remained before his death, and he was alone with the twelve disciples. There was no multitude in the background, and he asked them one question – *Who am I?* It is the ultimate question that every human must address: *Who is Jesus?*

Jesus prayed before he posed this all-important question (Luke 9:18). He knew that without revelation from the Father, it would be impossible for those men to believe that he was God. Put yourself in the place of those disciples. Jesus did not have a halo. There was no glow on his face. In fact, Isaiah said he had no exceptional beauty. Of course, he was full of love and goodness and they had been with him as he taught and healed, but he also ate, slept, and got tired. The incarnation is beyond human understanding, and so before Jesus asked the disciples who they thought he was, he prayed.

He asked: *Who do the people say the Son of Man is?* In effect, *Give me the result of the polls.*

The disciples decided to go with the more positive feedback they had heard. So, they told Jesus that the crowds knew there was something supernatural about him. The people identified him with the prophets of old, concluding that Jesus spoke for God as the prophets had. Many of them wanted to speak highly of Jesus without recognizing his deity and Lordship.

What does the crowd say about Jesus today? Many say that he was a good man. Some go so far as to say that he was probably the best man who ever lived. A great teacher, the founder of Christianity. Few acknowledge him as Lord and God.

Then Jesus posed a second question. He asked his disciples pointedly who *they* thought he was. "But who do you say that I am" (v.15)? Simon Peter, spokesman for the group, answered. His answer was brief and decisive: "You are the Christ, the Son of the living God." The Christ. Clearly he was referring to the Messiah, the Anointed One. The One who fulfilled all the promises and expectations given throughout thousands of years of Jewish history. Peter said in effect, *All of our prophets and leaders have spoken about you for centuries.* Peter called him the Son of the living God. Not just a prophet or teacher, but divine Son – God himself incarnate.

By God's revelation, Peter had come to understand in his heart of hearts that this was the One to whom all of history had been pointing – the only

Mediator between God and man. The Way, the Truth, and the Life, and no man could come to the Father except by him.

Jesus responded to Peter by saying: "Blessed are you, Simon Bar-Jonah! For flesh and blood has not revealed this to you, but my Father who is in heaven" (v.17). The human mind cannot grasp God's truth apart from the working of the Holy Spirit. We are meant to use our brains, but it is God's revelation that makes our hearts come alive, our understanding dawn, and our study fruitful.

If you side with the crowd, no matter how much you approve of Jesus as a moral and spiritual leader, you will be lost. If you say with Peter, "You are the Christ, the Son of the Living God" and follow him as such, you will experience salvation, passing from death to life! Like Peter, you too will be called blessed.

Day 19 – The Rock Becomes a Stumbling Block
Matthew 16:21-28

"From that time Jesus began to show his disciples that he must go to Jerusalem and suffer many things from the elders and chief priests and scribes, and be killed, and on the third day be raised. And Peter took him aside and began to rebuke him, saying, 'Far be it from you, Lord! This shall never happen to you.'" – Matthew 16:21-22

Peter had a revelation of Christ (v.13-20), but he had yet to understand the cross. He knew Jesus was to save the world, but he did not understand the means by which that would be accomplished. Not only did he not understand, but he attempted to squash the very idea that Jesus would die.

Sometimes we try to interfere when God is doing something hard in someone's life. Like Peter, instead of being a Rock, we inadvertently become a stumbling block.

Jesus cut Peter off abruptly and accused him of being a mouthpiece for the adversary. "Jesus turned and said to Peter, 'Get behind me, Satan! You are a hindrance to me. For you are not setting your mind on the things of God, but on the things of man'" (Matt. 16:23). It would be hard to imagine that anything could shock Peter more than those words.

The same apostle who just confessed Jesus as the Messiah quickly opposed his mission. Whatever spiritual experiences we may have had, let us not think that we can reach a spiritual plateau where we are forever insulated from sin and failure. Peter is a wonderful example of just how quickly we can move from being led by the Spirit to being led by the flesh in cahoots with the devil. A child of God cannot be possessed by Satan, but our words and actions can line up with his purposes instead of the Lord's.

Peter's intentions seemed honorable, loving, even compassionate. His concern for his own welfare is also understandable. He and the other disciples had given up everything for Jesus. Where would they be if Jesus died?

We rebuke Peter for his presumption, and yet we need to be honest about how we may have contradicted our Lord. How often do we argue when we have a clear word for our life in his Word? Or when the truth about his kingdom goes against what we expect or want to think? Where have you allowed your ideas, opinions, or plans to hinder Christ's goals for yourself or others?

Peter didn't err because he did not love Jesus. A love focused in the wrong direction is sometimes the cause of our hindering. Peter causes us to ask: Where am I tempting someone to reject God's will for his or her life because it involves suffering or sacrifice? This especially relates to our children. We may be hindering God's plan for their lives by over-protecting them or trying to make their lives too easy. Would you gladly send your children to the mission field if God calls them? Do not let your love for them keep them from God's best.

We need to realize that we are like Peter. Though we are privileged beyond compare to know the full gospel story, on a smaller scale, we have only heard or know part of the story of our lives. Peter was attempting to thwart the will of God, not realizing that what he was trying to stop would have eternal consequences for the entire world!

So, what can we do? We need God's insight. Jesus said that Peter was not setting his mind on God's interest, but man's. As Christians, we now have the mind of Christ, and the apostle Paul urges, "Do not be conformed to this world, but be transformed by the renewal of your mind, that by testing you may discern what is the will of God, what is good and acceptable and perfect" (Romans 12:2).

Peter had a tendency to argue with God's Word. He had enough faith to confess Jesus was the Son of God, but not enough to believe it was God's will for Jesus to suffer and die. It was just so utterly contrary to what he believed that he took the Lord aside and began to rebuke him! God's plan of salvation does not correspond to man's. Jesus is not the kind of Messiah man expects, and the person who insists on clinging to her own description of a Savior and coming to God on her own terms finds herself in opposition to God. Human nature always opposes the cross – both for Christ and for ourselves. Man's way never leads to the cross, and interference with the will of God is partnership with Satan.

Throughout Jesus' ministry, Satan tried to convince the Lord that he had a better idea than God did. Here he used Peter to say that God's plan was too difficult. The same Christian who once extolled the plan of God can be deceived into supporting the plan of the enemy. When we follow our own wisdom instead of the Spirit's, we unwittingly take Satan's side. When we trust our own perspective, we no longer see God's. When we focus on present pain or potential distress, rather than on the Lord, we are easy prey for the devil. We can even become traps that hinder another from following God's call. Let us not argue with the Word of God, even when it flies in the face of our expectations. And let us praise the Lord that his plan doesn't meet our expectations. In light of eternity, it far exceeds them!

Day 20 – Scars Before Glory
Matthew 16:24

"If anyone would come after me, let him deny himself and take up his cross and follow me.'"
–Matthew 16:24

If Jesus' disciples were overwhelmed by the fact that their Lord would die, how could they handle the assertion that they, too, must forget their own ambitions and accept a similar goal for themselves? Their thoughts quickly shifted from *"A cross for Christ?"* to *"A cross for me?"*

These verses describe the heart of Christian discipleship, and they strike a deathblow to self-centered false gospels - gospels that portray God as a genie who jumps to fulfill our every wish. Jesus never led anyone to think that following him would be easy, and we should never mislead others. Do not promise that it is easy, but by all means, declare that it is more than worth it!

God set the criteria for salvation and discipleship. For every believer, there is not only the initial call to come, but there is a call to follow in daily obedience to Christ. Jesus explains: We win by losing our life – by self-denial, cross-bearing, and loyal obedience. In order to find true fulfillment, we must deny ourselves, take up our cross, and follow Christ. Many want a "no cost discipleship," but Christ does not present that as an option. We need to understand that in losing our life for Jesus, we actually save it. We become what we were created to be. In dying, our true life comes forth.

What is our cross today? What is it that we are to "take up" on a daily basis? It is not the common trials and hardships all persons experience in life. Our cross is not the consequences of our own sin, not an unsaved husband, or a domineering mother-in-law. It is not even a physical handicap or suffering from a chronic disease. Taking up our cross is doing God's will when it crosses ours. It is being willing to obey at any price – giving up your will, your personal agenda, to walk in His – regardless of what it costs. It is willingness to endure shame, embarrassment, rejection, or even martyrdom for his sake.

Are you denying yourself, taking up your cross, and following him? Where are the marks of the cross in your body (Gal. 6:17)? Maybe you don't like to talk about them. Maybe few people even know about them, but you and he know they are there. Jesus is watching you and walking with you today as you bear the cross he has given you.

> Hast thou no scar, no hidden scar on feet or side or hand?
> I hear thee sung as mighty in the land.
> I hear them hail thee as a bright ascending star- but hast thou no scar?
> No wound, no scar? Yet as the Master shall the servant be – and pierced

are the feet that follow thee.
Can he have followed far who has no wound, no scar?

- Amy Carmichael

Day 21 – A Different Agenda
Matthew 17:1-13

At some point in his rise to prominence, Jesus took a fork in the road and never looked back. Up until then, followers rallied around him as he stood up to the city councils and bureaucrats. He boldly revealed the self-serving hypocrisy of the prominent men of the cloth. He talked with anybody, from common workers to elite civic leaders. From prostitutes to fishermen on the wharf. He gave stirring speeches about better days ahead and backed up his promises with solid performance. He could plunge into a crowd with the best of them, touching, teaching, filling needs.

Then, abruptly, his style changed. He started withdrawing with just a few of his inner circle, telling strange, at times incomprehensible stories – avoiding the very crowds that were longing to thrust him to the top. Although he was a young man barely in his prime, Jesus began to talk more and more about his death.

Jesus' disciples must have been blown away. Bewildered. Even Peter, one of the privileged inner circle, tried to stop all the illogical talk about betrayal, humiliation, and death. He was stunned when his Teacher issued a harsh reprimand. Jesus would have no political agendas pushed on him. From then on, he would seek to clarify the agenda of his Father.

At the same time, the Lord was aware that his men were bruised and shaken over the turn of events. They needed encouragement. So after more talk about taking up your cross and losing your life to find it, the Lord did something amazing.

Three men were able to see this powerful confirmation that Jesus is indeed the Messiah and is indeed God. It was the only time that his glory – that glory which Jesus had enjoyed with the Father even before creation – was allowed to fully shine forth while he was clothed in human flesh.

Matthew 17:2 tells us that Jesus was transfigured. He literally "changed form." The gospel writers tell us that his face shone like the sun. His clothes became as white as light. Everything else faded in his brilliance. The disciples saw the face of Jesus with the veil taken away, and its radiance was stunning. This was not a reflected radiance like Moses displayed after meeting with God on Mt. Sinai. Moses' face shone with borrowed light. Christ's face shone as the sun with inherent light.

We can imagine Jesus as the rugged man who walked the hills of Judea, but our minds are incapable of grasping the glorified Christ. No words can fully describe what the face of Christ must have looked like. But for that moment,

Jesus' body that was designed for time and space took on his eternal qualities and he shone with an incredible brightness.

John would again have a similar vision. While meditating on the isle of Patmos, he heard a voice. When he turned, there was a magnificent Person, and John wrote that his face shone like the sun. This man was Christ, Head of the Church. His glory was revealed also to Stephen at his death and to Saul on the Damascus road. One day, when he returns to reign forever, his glory will light up the whole world.

Those three disciples - Peter, James, and John – saw Jesus in his dazzling glory, and then they saw Moses and Elijah join him! We don't know how they identified Moses and Elijah. Maybe Jesus addressed them by name. Maybe they just intuitively recognized them. Nevertheless, they knew who they were – the Great Law Giver and the Great Prophet.

While Judaism was rejecting the Messiah, two of its most illustrious representatives were acknowledging and adoring him. The Old Covenant and the New Covenant met together on the mountain.

Why should these two come? For the disciples it was striking proof that his coming rejection and sufferings were perfectly consistent with the Messiah's purpose. They needed this proof, for though they were well versed in the thousands of Messianic prophecies, they had focused only on the Messiah's triumph and glory. They didn't realize that he had come to die. They thought that one day Jesus would take on the Romans, establish Israel, and lead them all to glory.

On the mount of transfiguration, God showed that Moses (representing the Law) and Elijah (representing the prophets) both spoke about the cross. The cross was in God's plan from the beginning. The law and the prophets continually promised better things than themselves, and on that mountain Jesus stood as the fulfillment of the law and the prophets. The eyes of believers should now and forever look to Jesus as the Author and Finisher of the faith.

Moses joined the ultimate Passover Lamb, the Lamb who would bring deliverance from sin and death for all who put their faith in him. Moses was there to bear witness that the perfect Passover Lamb would be slain. To testify that in the exodus Jesus would lead, a nobler rock would be smitten than the one he struck in the wilderness. A richer fountain would flow with living water.

Elijah bore witness that Christ's sacrifice would be greater than the one he laid on Mt. Carmel's altar. There would be a more wondrous confirmation than the fire that fell that day. In his case, there would be a glorious resurrection!

How good of God to offer such dazzling assurance to the disciples. It didn't sink in right away, but after Jesus' resurrection, such puzzle pieces began to fit together. The Lord's agenda became clear, and their lives were never the same.

Day 22 – A Little Child Shall Lead Them
Matthew 18:1-4

Have you ever dreamed of being great - of having real authority or position?

Christ's disciples did. They thought the Kingdom was coming in its fullness in their lifetime and wondered who would be the greatest when it did. This makes the disciples very relatable, very much like us. They had a knack for saying the wrong thing at the wrong time and asking the wrong questions because they were usually trying to solve the wrong problem.

Matthew 18 introduces a section of teaching that is all about personal relationships within the family of God. This section begins with the disciples' question about which of them would be the greatest in the kingdom of God.

Imagine how Jesus must have felt. He was dreading his betrayal and the cup he would drink, and not one disciple understood. Have you ever felt like that? – that nobody understands. Know that our Lord understands perfectly.

These men spent three years walking in the footsteps of the Living God, listening to him teach and preach, hearing his spiritual stories wrapped in practical packages, and they marveled. They saw him feed 5,000 men and their families with a boxed lunch. Then 4,000 more. They watched when he restored sight and caused the lame to walk. They saw his compassion as the multitudes pressed upon him and interrupted his plans. These men were on the ground with Jesus, yet the burning question in the minds of these spiritual giants was: *Which one of us is God's favorite?*

Standing in the shadows of humility personified, they wanted recognition. At the feet of the One who thought equality with God not a thing to be grasped, they asked to be as equal to God as possible. They missed the point, even though Jesus said it in so many ways.

He patiently decided to tell them again, this time by playing show and tell. Jesus loved to use wind and wheat and rocks and sand to teach. This time His object lesson was a little child.

In verses 2-3, Jesus knelt down, tenderly beckoned a little child, and answered his recognition-seeking followers: "Unless you change and become like little children, you will never enter the kingdom of heaven."

Notice that the Lord does not say to become *childish*, but to become as little children. He is not talking about reverting to childish behavior, but receiving new life with the faith of a child.

In effect, he said, *Fellows, you're trying to solve the wrong problems. You have natural, fleshly ambitions. You're trying to acquire position and prestige. Unless that attitude turns and you become like this child, you're not even going to make it into the kingdom you long to rule.* Pretty strong words for those who assumed not only entrance into the Kingdom but hierarchy within it.

Jesus emphasized the fact that a person must *enter* the Kingdom, which assumes that one is born outside of it. We are not born heavenly citizens. In such a way, the Lord diverted the disciples' attention from the matter of holding an exalted place in the Kingdom to that of primary importance – gaining entrance into it.

Think about the child Christ called as his living illustration. He came when Jesus called him. It's never really a problem to get young children to come to Christ. Instead, the problem is those who would keep them away. The child exemplified the dependence that we must have on Christ to be saved. A child instinctively trusts his parents to meet his needs. He cannot buy his own food or clothes, can't maintain his home, yet a loved child never doubts that he will be fed, clothed, and comforted. There is great dependence and trust in a little child.

Children have other remarkable qualities. One of their most beautiful qualities is that they like to be taught. The doors of their life are flung wide open to wonder. They gasp in surprise, laugh out loud, cry without shame. Children embrace mystery. They are helpless, simple, honest, believing, trusting. They have empty hands stretched out to receive.

Let little children remind you of the irony of God's plan – made so simple a child can understand, and such that the one who will not take on the mindset of a child cannot understand.

The Lord's invitation is to come to him humbly, receive him as your Savior, and be born again as a child of God. The Sermon on the Mount told us that those who recognize their own unworthiness are blessed. Come in your poverty to receive his grace and enter his kingdom with the faith and wonder of a child.

Day 23 – Two Become One
Matthew 19:1-12

Wherever Jesus was ministering, the scribes and Pharisees appeared. They came with their slick questions – not to play innocent games, but to take away his following and ultimately bring about his death.

In our passage today, they asked this question: "Is it lawful to divorce one's wife for any cause?" (v.3) Now, the Pharisees disagreed amongst themselves on the terms for divorce. In Deuteronomy 24:1, Moses said, "When a man takes a wife and marries her, if then she finds no favor in his eyes because he has found some indecency in her, and he writes her a certificate of divorce and puts it in her hand and sends her out of his house...." The Pharisees were divided on the phrase "some indecency." One school said that divorce was only allowed on the basis of immorality, and another school taught that anything a wife did that was offensive to her husband could qualify. If she put too much salt in his soup or talked too loudly, the husband had grounds for divorce. Believe it or not, this view was the most popular. The Pharisees thought that whatever answer Jesus gave would get him into trouble with someone. Today, divorce is still a topic of much contention and a painful thing to discuss. With that in mind, we come to this topic prayerfully and humbly to learn what God's best for marriage is.

Jesus answered the Pharisees' trick question by going straight to the Word. He quoted Genesis and said: "Have you not read that he who created them from the beginning made them male and female, and said, 'Therefore a man shall leave his father and his mother and hold fast to his wife, and the two shall become one flesh'? So they are no longer two but one flesh. What therefore God has joined together, let not man separate'" (19:4-6). In other words, He said: *Your argument isn't with me. Let me quote God on the subject.* When you and I are questioned on the subject of marriage, do we try to come up with our best logical argument, or do we point to God's revealed will in the Bible?

In pointing the religious leaders back to Genesis 1 and 2, Jesus reminds us of three crucial principles for marriage.

First, we are reminded that God designed marriage for one man and one woman. Male and female he created them. Both polygamy and homosexuality go against God's design for marriage. What is more, divorce was not an option for Adam; there were no alternatives to being faithful to Eve. God was creating a standard. Just because other choices came along in time didn't change God's intention.

Secondly, God instituted the leave and cleave principle. Neither Adam nor Eve had a mother or an earthly father, but God's Spirit was revealing an incredible plan for all generations. They were to establish a new family. Despite this principle, some do not ever really leave their parents emotionally, financially, or sometimes even physically. Of course, leaving and cleaving does not mean that you have nothing to do with your parents when you marry, but it does mean that you establish your own home and function as a separate entity. Marriage is to supersede the sacred relationship of parent and child. If a man or woman continues to consider the parents more significant than the marriage relationship, there is trouble. Love your parents. Honor them. But leave and cleave to your husband. Parents, let your children go to this new relationship. Any relationship that competes with or is in conflict with the husband-wife relationship is wrong. This means that we should be careful about spending time with other women who verbally tear down either their husbands or Scriptural principles about marriage. It means that you praise God for your husband's strengths instead of comparing him to someone else.

The third principle is that of the two becoming one flesh. This is not one dominating the other, nor is it two people setting up a 50-50 living arrangement. It is the picture of two so intermingled that we cannot tell where the fiber of one begins or ends. Two who are distinct individuals with different personalities and different gifts become one. God made them one, and Scripture says that what God has joined together, no man should separate.

Marriage is a profound mystery. Paul wrote in Ephesians 5 that marriage is the picture that God chose to reflect his relationship with the church. What a precious picture of our relationship with Christ, and what value it gives to the marriage relationship.

Marriage is a picture of unbroken oneness, sacrificial love, and beautiful submission. Christ loved the church so much that he gave his life for her, but his death was not the end. It was the beginning of a renewed relationship with his people, and he promises: "I will never leave you nor forsake you" (Hebrews 13:5). Christ is forever faithful. This is God's ideal for marriage.

Day 24 – All of Grace
Matthew 20:1-16

The circumstances surrounding this parable would have been very familiar to the disciples. For about two weeks in Palestine, the grape harvest was at its peak to be harvested or else spoil. The landowners needed extra help, and the poor came to find work in this open market.

The owner of the vineyard represents God who calls laborers to help him harvest souls. He called some early in the morning around 6 a.m. He hired more at 9 a.m., 3 p.m., and just before the day ended, at 5 p.m.

He promised those he hired at 6 a.m. a denarius for the day's work. To the others, he did not say what he would give, just that it would be what was right. To the dismay of those hired early, at the end of the day they all got the same wage – a denarius.

What unexpected generosity! This owner had his own way of doing things. As Isaiah tells us, God's ways are not our ways. Not only did the owner give the latecomers the same wages, but he paid them in front of those who had worked all day. If he hadn't paid the latecomers first, the early ones wouldn't have seen what he gave the last, and they would have been grateful – for he gave them exactly what was promised.

The point of the story is quite plainly the scandal of grace – amazing grace! All are equally undeserving of the large sum of a denarius for a day. Everyone was paid quite generously.

Nobody can claim deserved membership in the Kingdom. There is no place for personal pride, contempt, or jealousy of others. There are no grounds to question how this generous God handles the utterly undeserving. The gift of God does not depend on human merit in any way whatsoever. It is the sheer grace of the Only One who is ultimately good and who accepts those who could never be good. Then, our good works spring from the life we have been given and are our grateful response to God's generosity.

We need to be careful not to watch God's other workers and measure ourselves by them – or criticize God for what he does for them. Unfortunately, the first workers in the parable saw the generosity given to the latecomers and asked, *Why didn't he give us more?* In verse 15, the owner said to the unhappy workers, *Don't I have a right to do what I want with my own?*

It is God's sovereign right to do what he wills in all things. It is not for us to question his choice of laborers or their reward. It follows then that he has a right to do what he wants with you and me. We are his, but sometimes we are afraid to trust the Lord. We fear what he might ask of us and wonder if he really is just in his assignments and his wages. Rest assured that God will give what is best, and know that he doesn't want us idle. His vineyard has a position for you and for me.

None of us ultimately receive what we deserve, because Jesus gave up his rights for us. He emptied himself so that we could receive that which is his by right. We do not want what we really deserve!

Despite this, the reaction of the first workers is very natural. Most of us have a hard time with this parable because we instinctively identify with the workers who worked all day instead of with those who worked only one hour. Those who came at the end of the shift were elated and grateful. They didn't think about unfairness; they considered the owner extremely gracious.

Usually we look around at others, instead of at Jesus, and we begin to feel pretty good about ourselves. We feel that we are the twelve-hour workers and remind God of the sacrifices we have made to serve him – perhaps even suggesting to God that we deserve x, y, or z.

As sovereign Ruler of the universe, God has the right to require and expect perfect, faithful service from all of us without any obligation on his part. He said to Job, "Who has first given to me, that I should repay him? Whatever is under the whole heaven is mine" (Job 41:11). In this instance, God was rebuking the attitude of entitlement. Paul wrote in Romans 11:35, "Or who has given a gift to him that he might be repaid?" As it has been so aptly said, "God is no man's debtor."

People have a sense of being owed something. Older people feel entitled to a comfortable life, middle-aged feel entitled to their benefits, and young people feel entitled to all that their parents have. However, that attitude is detrimental to society and totally out of line when it is examined in light of God's gracious gift of eternal life in Christ.

There are people who have known and served the Lord from an early age. They grew up in a Christian home and responded early in life to Jesus' call. There is also an older person in prison who might be even now responding to God's call for the first time. At various hours of life's day, people hear the call, enter into God's vineyard, and go to work for him. It is not the amount of time you serve, or the prominence or difficulty of the tasks that merit eternal life. The Lord doesn't give us himself or the riches of life in Christ because we worked a whole day or an hour. It is all of grace.

When we doubt the justice of God, it is always because our view of God and of ourselves has been distorted. God is the standard of righteousness, and it is impossible for him to be unjust. This parable is an illustration of the kingdom where God sovereignly reigns in both righteousness and grace. He alone establishes the terms of salvation, and his gift is not based on our merit. It is based upon his grace dispensed sovereignly and impartially to whomever he calls – no matter the time of day.

Day 25 – What Will You Do with the Son?
Matthew 21:33-45

The parable of the tenants was not a cryptic one. The religious leaders certainly understood Jesus' meaning, as he drew heavily upon Isaiah 5:1-7, which describes Israel as God's vineyard. This was a daring story that described Israel's scribes and Pharisees as greedy and even evil servants. Jesus used this parable to further answer their question about his authority saying, *I am the Beloved Son whom the Father has sent.*

The characters in the story would have been easy to identify. The vineyard was Israel, the owner God, the cultivators the religious leaders, and the messengers the prophets throughout history. Jesus is the beloved Son that the Owner sent to collect his harvest.

Notice that the owner ensured that everything possible was done to guarantee abundant fruit at harvest time. He put a wall around the vineyard to keep out wild animals and thieves, erected a tower for the watchman, and put in a winepress. Everything was ready, and he was expectant.

In the same way, God gave Israel every advantage by supplying them with all that they needed to be a godly nation. He conquered their enemies and placed them in a land flowing with milk and honey. He sent them judges and kings and his very Word for their instruction. He did all this that they might be healthy vines and produce much fruit.

In the parable, the owner left others to care for his vineyard. That frequently occurred in the ancient world, and likewise God gave the responsibility of caring for his people to the priests, elders, and scribes.

It was also common back then for the owner to send servants to collect his harvest. God sent his prophets through the ages – Isaiah, Jeremiah, and many others. These messengers were beaten and even killed.

In the story, the owner finally sends his beloved and only son. The tenants do not even respect him; in fact, they killed him. It was not a case of mistaken identity. They knew exactly who he was.

God expects reverence for and obedience to his Son. But, even today, people try to get rid of Jesus when he stands in the way of their selfish fulfillment. When we refuse him as Lord, we are declaring, *I am my own master. Everything really belongs to me.* The religious leaders did not want to acknowledge God's ownership. Too often we have the same problem, because we want to run things our way. Never mind that Jesus has every claim on our total allegiance. Never mind that he would make better, wiser choices that are truly for our good.

Jesus finished the parable by posing a question: "When therefore the owner of the vineyard comes, what will he do to those tenants" (v.40)? Jesus allowed the leaders to finish the story, asking them to be the judges. Jesus baited the trap, and they spoke their own condemnation: "He will put those wretches to a miserable death and let out the vineyard to other tenants who will give him the fruits in their seasons" (v.41).

So Jesus said to the elders and teachers of the law, "Therefore I tell you, the kingdom of God will be taken away from you and given to a people producing its fruits" (v.43). We know that within a short time, Jesus' words came true. The nation of Israel was lost both physically and spiritually. Jerusalem burned to the ground and the responsibility of the Kingdom was entrusted to the worldwide church.

God trusts men and women with his work. It is a great privilege to be given work in God's vineyard, but a servant must prove faithful – a far cry from the servants pictured here. God has provided for us just as bountifully as he did for Israel – even more so through Christ! We have the Holy Spirit indwelling our hearts and the whole of Scripture illuminating our way. He has given us all we need to be servants who bear much fruit (2 Peter 1:3-8). It is not as though we have to grow the fruit ourselves. His life flows through us and produces the fruit. He is the Vine; we are the branches (John 15).

The difference between being servants who greedily grasp for the harvest and servants who offer much fruit to the Owner of the vineyard lies in our response to His Son.

Day 26 – The Source of Love
Matthew 22:34-40

This is the fourth question in a series of trick questions. An expert of the law asked Jesus: "Teacher, which is the greatest commandment in the Law?"

We would do well to listen closely to his answer, for Jesus gives us what should be our number one priority. "You shall love the Lord your God with all your heart and with all your soul and with all your mind" (v.37).

In this instance, Jesus again appealed to Scripture for his answer to their question – this time going to Deuteronomy 6:5, the first text that every Jewish child learned. It was also the opening passage for every Jewish service. Jesus quoted a Scripture familiar to everyone as *the* greatest commandment, and it is the principle behind all of the other commandments.

When you are troubled and don't know what steps to take, begin with loving God. That is our highest calling. We have to admit that we seldom start with loving God. Almost always, we start by scrutinizing the demands upon us, instead of looking to the God who will lead us through the trial and asking how we can best glorify him in it. We can become so wrapped up with the problem that we can't get our minds off of it and onto God. But, if you start with loving God, the One who sees every angle of every problem will be your Help.

To be clear, something does in fact precede our loving God – and that is knowing that God loves us already. The command to love the Lord our God is impossible until we see that God has first loved us in Christ and that our love is a response to his. Just faced with a command to love a detached God up there somewhere, we would find it difficult to respond. But, as John put it in 1 John 4:19, "We love because he first loved us." It is God's Spirit who reveals his love to us and enables us to return that love.

When we know that his love redeemed us by giving his only Beloved Son, the only proper response is to love God back with all of our hearts, all of our souls, and all of our minds. This means that we observe and understand the truth of God's love, allow it to touch our emotions and move our will until finally, the whole body is engaged. Every part of our being is involved in loving God. God requires more than mere intellectual assent to him as Savior. James tells us that even the demons believe that God exists. But, instead of loving God back because of their belief, they shudder. The distinguishing mark of saving belief in God is love for God.

After giving the first and greatest commandment, Jesus added the second. "And a second is like it: You shall love your neighbor as yourself" (v.39). The second greatest commandment actually flows out of the first. Our response to God's love makes it possible for us to show our husband, children, neighbor,

52

friend, boss, etc. the same love we have received. We start with God's love and then pass it along. We cannot start with loving our neighbor apart from loving God first.

Love is not just a word to write on a plaque; it is what we do when people irritate us, when we are upset, angry, and feel like striking back. Begin with God – remembering his love for you and how he forgives all your sin out of the riches of his grace. Respond to this amazing love, and then you will be able to pass it on.

Love is active, not merely sentimental and emotional. Jesus said to love others as we love ourselves. When you are hungry, you feed yourself. When you are thirsty, you get yourself a drink. When you are sick, you take medicine or see a doctor. You care for yourself and do what is necessary to provide for yourself. We do not merely talk about our needs; we do something about them. That is how we are to respond to others in love.

God knows we need much love, and he gives us people to love us. We must know, however, that people alone are never an adequate source of love. God never intended them to be. If we depend upon people to meet our love need, we will be dissatisfied. God is the One who loves us completely and fully satisfies. His love alone meets the deepest needs of our heart, and it is from his love as displayed in the Gospel that our love for him and others flows.

Day 27 – Ready or Not, Here He Comes
Matthew 25:1-13

In this parable, the Lord warns of the danger of deluding ourselves about our readiness for his return. He exhorts us to be sure that we are prepared for his coming.

Weddings never go out of style. We make a great fuss over the bride. But in this parable, Jesus doesn't even mention the bride. His attention is focused on ten young ladies invited to the wedding and on the Bridegroom.

The backdrop is an eastern wedding, held at night and where it was customary for the bridegroom to go to the house of the bride and escort her to the wedding. As they walked through the streets, the couple would be joined by guests at various places along the route. Our Lord's story is of such a group of guests waiting for the bridegroom. This parable is not an allegory. In other words, not every facet of the story carries a spiritual meaning, but the story was told to emphasize one major point.

All ten virgins were waiting for the coming of the bridegroom, and though united in their expectation, they were quite divided in the way that they prepared. All ten took lamps. All professed to be participating in the ceremony and to love the prospect of his coming. As they waited, the ten were indistinguishable in appearance. But they were not truly alike.

The Bible says that five were foolish and five were wise. The foolish took lamps but did not take any oil with them. There was nothing to burn in their lamps that would give light. The wise took oil in jars along with their lamps.

The oil is a significant part of the story, yet it was trivial to the five foolish maidens. Oil is continuously used in Scripture to symbolize the power and Person of the Holy Spirit, whose presence differentiates the mere professing Christian from the one who is truly indwelt by the Living God. Both the wise and the foolish are still among the church. Even though we agree that we desire the Bridegroom to come, some are lacking what is essential to join the wedding feast.

As the young ladies waited, all ten grew weary and fell asleep. Suddenly, they heard the cry they had all been waiting for: "Here is the bridegroom! Come out to meet him" (v.6). We come to the crisis of the story when the foolish discover that their lamps are going out. This parable is directed to the professors who are not possessors. In the organized church today, we have many members – their names on the roll, baptized even, who have a feeling of being attached to Christ, but who do not possess the Holy Spirit as a seal and a guarantee of their entrance into the most extravagant wedding feast of all time.

The virgins who were ready went in to the celebration with the bridegroom, and the door was shut. This parable makes vividly clear the folly of being satisfied with an outward form of godliness. We have heard the Bridegroom's call loudly and plainly. Let us not depend upon our weak and very finite light to illumine our way. The Light of the World must live in our hearts and rule our lives. This is what makes one wise, and this is readiness.

Day 28 – Praiseworthy Extravagance
Matthew 26:6-13

Mary apparently knew Jesus better than most. John's gospel clues us in to the fact that the Mary in this story is the same Mary who was the sister of Martha and Lazarus. Earlier in Matthew, we read about Mary sitting at Jesus' feet and hanging onto his every word. The account in Luke tells us that Mary chose "the good part," that which could not be taken away, when she decided to spend her time sitting at the Lord's feet. Consequently, she knew him well and loved him.

In this chapter of Matthew, Mary poured out her love for the Lord in the best way she knew how. She took her jar of perfume and poured it out over his head and his feet. Then, she took her hair and wiped his feet with it. She anointed him with the most valuable possession she had, worth a year's wages. She may have been keeping this for her wedding or as security in case she never married. But, she gave Jesus her most treasured possession because she loved him and was sensitive to his need at this time. This was an extravagant gesture, criticized by some and yet applauded by the Lord.

Mary performed this act of love in front of everyone else at the meal; she didn't concern herself with what they might think of her. She simply poured out her love in full view. She was not a secret worshipper of God. She would not have been embarrassed to bow her head to pray in a restaurant. Mary's act was saying in essence: *I love him, and I know what's ahead.* She believed what he said about his upcoming death. She didn't understand everything, but what she did understand led her to this loving act.

Mary is an example to us to give our all in response to God's love and forgiveness. It is foolish-looking to the world. Think of the wise men who went to worship the infant King. Imagine those three lovely chests containing gold, frankincense, and myrrh sitting on the floor of that humble Bethlehem home. Did that make sense? Did the child even know that they were there? Was it a waste? How about the disciples? They too laid down what they had and left familiar fishing nets in a heap on the shore. They left behind their business and their family and friends to follow a man they barely knew. Where were they going? What were they going to do? What did it mean to fish for men anyway?

I am discovering more and more that when I'm willing to trust God and follow him – to do what I believe he is asking me to do – it doesn't have to make sense. It may look foolish. He is constantly leading me off the map, away from seeming security and into deeper trust.

God's ways are not limited by our reason or necessarily in line with earthly plans or even economics. Extravagance and costly obedience are part of his plan for our lives. Keep in mind who you are serving, and when he says "*Follow me,*" nothing will be too great to give up for the privilege. Mary illustrates for us how we should respond to the Son of God – with unself-conscious devotion and love. This kind of extravagant, praiseworthy love is born out of sitting at his feet.

Day 29 – Seeing Through the Cross
Matthew 26:47-56

The Lord was exhausted by his tremendous struggle in the Garden of Gethsemane. There were streaks of bloody perspiration on his face. Yet, victorious in his surrender to the Father, Jesus rose to face his accusers with a surprising peace. He relinquished his will and resolved to finish the mission appointed for him by God.

Jesus found his disciples sleeping and awakened them, saying: "Rise, let us be going; see, my betrayer is at hand" (v.46). Picture the scene. The green olive trees were outlined by the Passover moon shedding its quiet light, when suddenly, the quiet is shattered and the light of the moon is now reflected off of swords and spears in the hands of the soldiers coming for Jesus. Judas was at the head of the group, and he greeted Jesus with a double-crossing kiss on the cheek.

Jesus looked at him and said, "Friend, do what you came to do" (v.50). We immediately see that Judas isn't in charge at all. The Lord is in charge. He has been in control all along.

At this point, Peter took matters into his own hands, and his slashing sword cut off the ear of the high priest's servant. Jesus rebuked Peter, saying he could call down thousands upon thousands of angels to fight for him if he so desired. But, he would not. He was fulfilling his purpose – seeking and saving the lost. Jesus addressed the crowd with dignity: "Day after day I sat in the temple teaching, and you did not seize me. But all this has taken place that the Scriptures of the prophets might be fulfilled" (v.55-56). He was fully aware that he did not have to go with the soldiers; he had escaped mobs before. But now it was God's time, and his prayerful surrender in the Garden gave him a firm resolve.

It can be easy for you and me, moved by some emotion, to privately or publicly surrender to the Lord. Yet, even heartfelt surrender is meaningless unless it is accompanied by firm resolve that leads to action. Jesus continued to choose his Father's will when the circumstances became difficult. And so, our redemption graciously proceeded on schedule.

Peter swung his sword with good intentions. He wanted to help the Lord, but his actions could have resulted in his own death and the deaths of the other disciples. He was so far from understanding the Lord's will here that he could have caused quite a tragedy by his impulsiveness.

This is a lesson for you and me. We may be very devoted to the Lord, but we need to understand his mind. Often when we love people, we give them what we think they want or what we want to give them – not necessarily what the Lord has in mind. We need to read his Word to understand his mind so that we don't move apart from his will. Peter wasn't in tune with his Lord, so his devotion took a wrong turn. When we move according to the flesh, we always lop off ears.

Though Jesus had demonstrated his authority and majesty, the disciples and others were only aware of his humiliation as the soldiersroughly grabbed him and bound his hands with cords. Jesus Christ, who created and sustained the universe, humbled himself as a man in order to lift us up. In order to save us, he allowed men to humiliate him, treat him like a prisoner, and even kill him.

Jesus took the cup the Father had given him for the joy set before him (Hebrews 12:2). He despised the cross, Hebrews tells us, and looked beyond it to his resurrection and our redemption. As a follower of Jesus, when God gives you a cup that seems bitter, remember that he will follow it up with resurrection and glory (Romans 8). Your lips may be puckered right now as you try to down a sour cup. Fix your eyes on him who endured the cross and on the prize that makes our cross pale in comparison.

Day 30 – The Priest and the Lamb
Matthew 27:27-31

Then the soldiers of the governor took Jesus into the governor's headquarters, and they gathered the whole battalion before him. And they stripped him and put a scarlet robe on him, and twisting together a crown of thorns, they put it on his head and put a reed in his right hand. - Matthew 27:27-29a

When God originally cursed the earth for man's sin, he caused thorns and thistles to come forth from the ground. The thorn – the fruit of the curse – was pressed into Jesus' head. Jesus was made a curse for us who were otherwise helpless to come out from under the curse.

Then, the soldiers put a staff in his right head, knelt in front of him, and mocked him saying, "Hail, King of the Jews!" They went so far as to spit on him and strike him again and again. The rough, hard-handed soldiers were accustomed to carrying out gruesome orders, but now they were also having a bit of sport with the Lord of the universe. To them, he was of no special significance. They began playing with him, running with the idea that he claimed to be king of the Jews. After all, they as Romans were the rulers of this obscure little country. So, they poked fun at Jesus. To the soldiers it was all a joke that this meek, seemingly defenseless prisoner should ever have imagined himself or permitted his followers to think of him as a king. In their eyes, there was nothing regal about him. Yet, to the eyes of faith, Jesus was never more royal than when he endured such scorn and mistreatment with holy patience and submission to the Father's will. Jesus is King over all, whether any person declares him so or not. God has declared it, and his purposes stand forever.

Once the soldiers wearied of the vulgar treatment, they led Jesus away to be crucified. He was led outside the walls of the holy city to be crucified as a common criminal. Jesus loved Jerusalem. He was King of Jerusalem whether they acknowledged it or not, and he had wept for this city. Nevertheless, David's city was so far removed from David's Lord that she cast out his greatest Son as an unclean thing.

Long ago and in many ways, God had foreshadowed the sacrifice Jesus would make and the rejection he would suffer. He commanded his people to sacrifice a perfect lamb as payment for their sins. Under the guidance of the priest, the man would place his hands on the head of the lamb and confess his sins. Symbolically, the sin passed from the person to the lamb. The person that sinned then killed the lamb, and the priest took the blood of the lamb and put it on the altar. The carcass of a sin offering lamb was then taken *outside* the camp and burned as unclean, for it bore the man's sins.

The book of Hebrews tells us that the Old Testament observances were shadows that pointed toward Jesus' once-and-for-all sacrifice. He was taken outside the city of Jerusalem and put to death, carrying my sins and yours. He was made sin for us. The perfect, holy Son of God became unclean because he carried my rebellion, self-will, jealousy, pride, bitterness, love of self, and ugly words. Understand that every one of our personal sins were on him that day. He was treated as unclean that you and I might be clean before God! He was cast out that those of us once alienated from God, might never be cast out of his presence again. The Lord Jesus was made sin for you and I. He endured the humiliation and all the agony that we might become the righteousness of God in him. Praise the Lord.

Day 31 – From Hiding to Heralding
Matthew 28

As the sun rose on the first day of the week, a new age dawned. A group of women went to the tomb, hearts heavy with grief and bringing spices they had prepared for Jesus' body. The resurrection was far from their thoughts. All their hopes and dreams had come to an end with the death of their Lord. Now, their concern was over who would roll away the stone from the entrance to the tomb.

They were unaware that a second earthquake had shaken the grave where Jesus had been laid. At his death, the world trembled with fear, and at his resurrection it quaked with joy! The stone was not removed for the Lord to get out of the tomb, but for the women and his disciples to peer in.

Despite the fact that Jesus' followers did not go to the tomb expecting the resurrection he had prophesied, God used an angel to speak words of comfort to them. The angel said, "Do not be afraid, for I know that you seek Jesus who was crucified. He is not here, for he is risen, as he said. Come, see the place where he lay..." (Matthew 28:5-6). God turned the sorrow of these women into joy. Women were counted for very little in those days. They could not even witness in a court of law. If anyone were going to fabricate the story of the resurrection, they would not have designated women to be the witnesses. Only God could have dreamed up such a remarkable thing. After God does his greatest act, raising his Son from the dead, he attests to it through the lips of those so widely discounted. God's Word tells us that he chooses the weak to confound the strong; how magnificent!

The women were to share the wonderful news immediately. "But go, tell his disciples and Peter," Mark recorded (Mark 16:7). "And Peter" - what a tender touch, a gentle word. The last we saw of Peter, he was weeping bitterly in the night after his denial. Now, Jesus specifically embraced him. Jesus cares for his followers as individuals, even individuals who fail. He delights to restore us to himself.

In Matthew 28:9, the women hurried away from the tomb, afraid yet filled with joy. Suddenly, Jesus met them. At this point they had heard the angel's proclamation, seen the empty tomb, and beheld the risen Lord. They could do nothing but adore him. Adoration and praise are the only proper responses to his presence. They did what every person, believer or unbeliever will do when the Lord comes again – they bowed their knees.

Jesus commanded the women, "Do not be afraid; go and tell my brothers to go to Galilee, and there they will see me" (Matthew 28:10). It would have seemed justified if the Lord had allowed the disciples to suffer in fear and despair for a week or so before telling them the good news. But, in his gracious mercy,

Jesus sent word to the disciples as soon as possible. He did not rebuke them for their lack of faith or their cowardice. Instead, he sent messengers with hope, comfort, and a new command. The command to go to Galilee would lead to a new commission, a commission that still drives us, and to the promise of his presence that still strengthens us to obey.

"Now the eleven disciples went to Galilee, to the mountain to which Jesus had directed them. And when they saw him they worshipped him, but some doubted. And Jesus came and said to them, 'All authority in heaven and on earth has been given to me. Go therefore and make disciples of all nations, baptizing them in the name of the Father and of the Son and of the Holy Spirit, teaching them to observe all that I have commanded you. And behold, I am with you always, to the end of the age." -Matthew 28:16-20

Christian, this is your King.